# unbelievably BAD jokes

THE BEANObooks
geddes & grosset

2

Why do Plug's ears stick out so far?

Well, if you were Plug's ears, wouldn't you want to be as far away as possible from him?

What do you get if you cross a frog and a dog?

A croaker Spaniel!

● ● ● ●

What's green and square?

An orange in disguise!

3

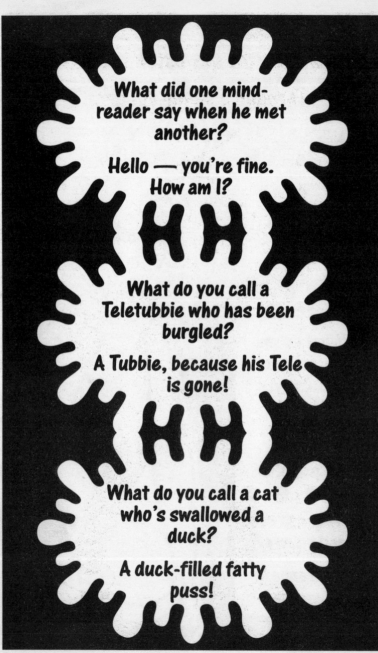

What did one mind-reader say when he met another?

Hello — you're fine. How am I?

What do you call a Teletubbie who has been burgled?

A Tubbie, because his Tele is gone!

What do you call a cat who's swallowed a duck?

A duck-filled fatty puss!

How does the sky listen to music?

Through a cloud-speaker.

What's Billy Whizz's favourite flavour of crisp?

Cheese and RUN-ION!

5

6

What do you get if you cross a shark with a snowman?

Frostbite!

● ● ● ● ● ● ● ● ● ● ● ●

Where does a frog hang its coat?

In a croakroom!

● ● ● ● ● ● ● ● ● ● ● ●

When is it Luke Skywalker's birthday?

May the Fourth (be with you!).

Teacher — How do you catch a rabbit?

Smiffy — Hide behind a tree and make a noise like a carrot!

What's the difference between a hot dog and a cold dog?

A hot dog goes "Grr" . . .
. . . and a cold dog goes "BRR"!

What's the best thing to put in a sandwich?

Your teeth!

Why can you run faster when you have a cold?

I don't know!

Because your pulse races and your nose runs!

That dog bit my leg.
Did you put anything on it?

No, he liked it just the way it was.

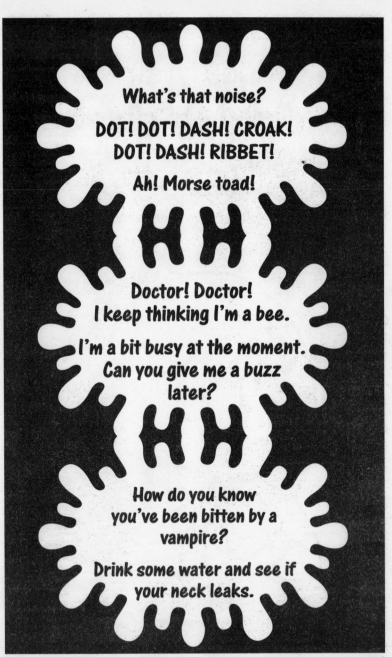

What's that noise?

DOT! DOT! DASH! CROAK!
DOT! DASH! RIBBET!

Ah! Morse toad!

Doctor! Doctor!
I keep thinking I'm a bee.

I'm a bit busy at the moment.
Can you give me a buzz
later?

How do you know
you've been bitten by a
vampire?

Drink some water and see if
your neck leaks.

What subject do insects prefer at school?

Mothematics!

● ● ● ● ● ● ● ● ● ● ● ●

What is the lowest common denominator?

Gosh! Hasn't anyone found it yet?
They were looking for that when I
was at school.

12

What's a spider's favourite food?

French flies!

● ● ● ● ● ● ● ● ●

How do you set up a flea circus?

From scratch!

● ● ● ● ● ● ● ● ●

What kind of bow is it impossible to tie?

A rainbow.

23

Which animal should you take with you on a day out in the country?

A picnic hamster!

How do lions, tigers and elephants fly?

On the African PLANE!

What did one Highland cow say to the other?

Och, aye the MOO!

Why did the boy cross the playground?

To get to the other slide!

● ● ● ● ● ● ● ● ● ● ●

Why didn't Rasher play football?

Because he pulled his hamstring!

● ● ● ● ● ● ● ● ● ● ●

What's yellow and grows in an apple tree?

A stupid banana.

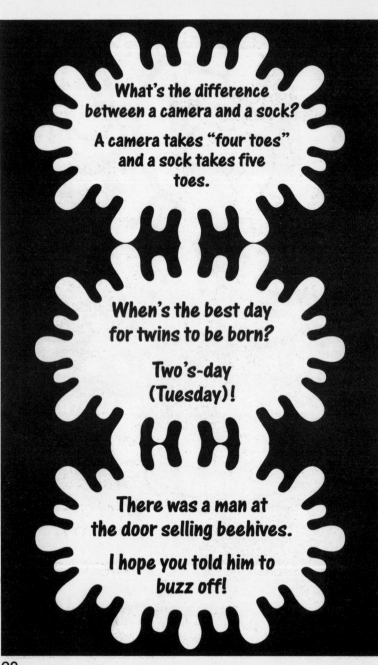

What's the difference between a camera and a sock?

A camera takes "four toes" and a sock takes five toes.

When's the best day for twins to be born?

Two's-day (Tuesday)!

There was a man at the door selling beehives.

I hope you told him to buzz off!

What do you call a rich bear?

Winnie the Pools!

• • • •

What's got a long tongue and walks a yellow brick road?

The Lizard of Oz.

• • • •

Where do they make car horns?

Hong-King!

**What do swamp monsters like for their tea?**

**Beings on toast!**

● ● ● ● ● ● ● ●

**What do jelly babies wear on their feet?**
**Gumboots!**

**What martial art makes you lie in bed?**

Kung-FLU!

● ● ● ●

**What was Noah's profession?**

ARK-itect.

● ● ● ●

**What's green, covered in custard, and miserable?**

Apple grumble!

● ● ●

**What does a cat sleep on?**

A caterpillow!

**Why did the farmer drive a steamroller through his fields?**

**He wanted to grow mashed potatoes!**

● ● ● ● ● ● ● ● ● ● ●

**What are pink, white, sing in a high voice and come out at night?**

**Falsetto teeth!**

How do you make a band stand?

Hide all the chairs!

Who ate his victims two by two?

Noah shark!

What has four legs and can fly?

Two birds!

What kind of dance do cows go to?

A barn dance!

Doctor, doctor. I swallowed a trumpet.

I'd better take some notes.

● ● ● ● ● ● ● ● ●

Why did the thief steal a box of soap?

He wanted to make a clean getaway.

Doctor, Doctor, my little boy's swallowed a bullet!

Well, don't point him at me!

Why did the teacher have to wear sunglasses?

Because his pupils were so bright.

Why do we plant bulbs in the garden?

So the worms can see where they're going!

What's this frog doing in my alphabet soup?

Learning to read!

● ● ● ● ● ● ● ● ●

What's a penguin's favourite sport?

South Pole vaulting!

● ● ● ● ● ● ● ● ●

How d'you raise an abandoned elephant?

With a fork-lift truck!

41

45

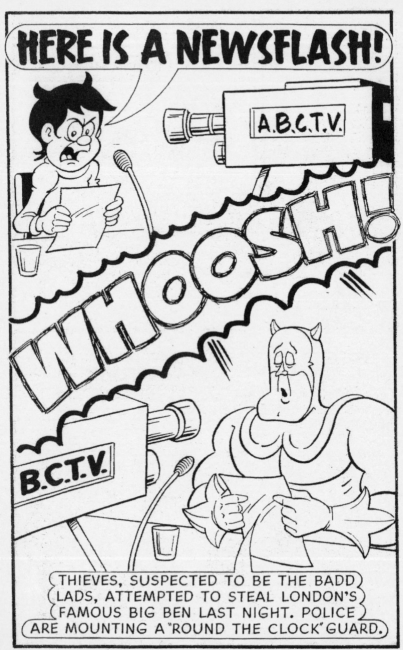

48

What's big and grey and wears a mask?

The Elephantom Of The Opera!

What's tall and hairy and can drive faster than anybody else?

Michael Chewbacca!

What opens doors and buzzes?

A Bumble Key!

What's 300m tall and attracts bees?

The Eiffel FLOWER!

What do you get if it rains cats and dogs?

A poodle!

Who gave you that black eye, Smiffy?

Nobody, I had to fight for it!

What happened to the gardeners' football team when one of them was injured?

They brought on a shrubstitute!

What vegetable is handy on a building site?

A wheel-MARROW!

**What time do ducks get up?**

**At the quack of dawn!**

● ● ● ● ● ● ● ● ●

**What's green, spiky and hops?**

**A hedgefrog!**

**What's the difference between African and Indian elephants?**

**About three thousand miles!**

● ● ● ● ● ● ● ●

**When do kangaroos go on holiday?**

**Spring!**

● ● ● ● ● ● ● ●

**Where do vampires have their hair cut?**

**The scare dressers!**

What does the sea say to the beach?

Nothing — it waves!

● ● ● ● ● ● ● ● ●

Where do frogs borrow money?

From a river bank!

What happened to the man who stole some pudding?

He was put in "custardy"!

● ● ● ● ● ● ● ● ● ● ●

Why do bananas put on suntan oil?

Because they peel!

**Why is it silly to break into a bank?**

**Because it's full of coppers!**

**What did Mum Glo-worm say to Dad Glo-worm?**

**Isn't our son bright for his age!**

**What do birds use for emergency landings?**
**Sparrow-chutes!**

●●●●●●●●●●

**What is a ghost's favourite fun-fair ride?**
**A roller-ghoster!**

●●●●●●●●●

**Did you hear about the fly in the butter?**
**Yes — it was a butterfly!**

Where do cows go
for entertainment?

The moo-vies!

Where is the silliest
place on Earth?

Twitzerland!

What do pigs use to
write to their friends?

Pen . . . and oink!

Do you think clumsiness is catching?

No — I think it's dropping!

What's a swamp monster's favourite drink?

Slime cordial!

Why does a bald man have no use for keys?

Because he's lost his locks!

● ● ● ● ● ● ● ● ●

Why do bees hum?

Because they can't remember the words.

62

68

69

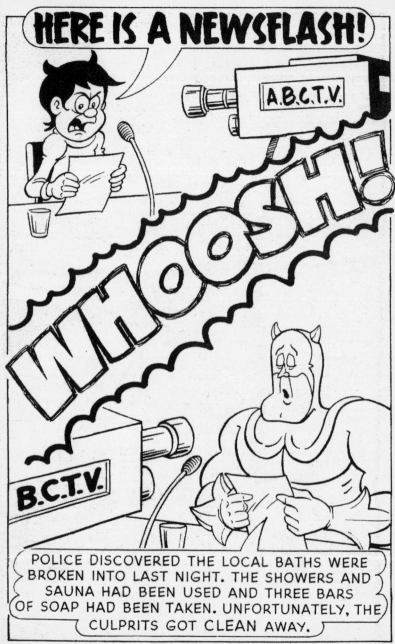

What goes ring-WOBBLE! Ring-WOBBLE!
A jellyphone!

What do lady sheep wear?
Ewe-niforms!

Why can't leopards escape from zoos?

Because they're always spotted!

● ● ● ● ● ● ● ● ● ● ● ●

What's a prickly "pair"?

Two hedgehogs!

What does a stupid monkey wear in cold weather?

A chumper!

What happened to the cat who swallowed a ball of wool?

She had mittens.

What do you call a one-eyed dinosaur?

A Dyouthinkesawrus!

What's a cat's favourite holiday resort?

The Canary Islands.

● ● ● ● ● ● ● ● ● ●

Why do bees have sticky hair?

Because they have honey combs.

LITTER

CUTHBERT
CRINGEWORTHY

**What did the traffic warden have on his sandwiches?**

**Traffic jam.**

● ● ● ● ● ● ● ● ●

**What do you call a horse that's been all round the world?**

**A globe-trotter.**

**What does Farmer Duck drive?**

**A quack-tor.**

● ● ● ● ● ● ● ● ● ● ● ●

**What's white on the outside and tells terrible jokes?**

**A corny beef sandwich.**

What do bees say in summer?
"'Swarm".

●●●●●●●●●

What do you call five bottles of lemonade?
A pop group.

●●●●●●●●●

Where do bulls go on holiday?
Bull-garia.

(Two figures in plane)
Are we going to fall out?

No — we'll still be friends.

What do you do when the M6 is closed?

Go up the M3 twice!

Who's there?
Dwane.
Dwane who?

Dwane the bath
— I'm drowning!

What do you get if you cross a dog with a phone?

A golden receiver!

What is a zebra?

A horse too lazy to take off his pyjamas.

What fruit do vampire bats like best?

Blood oranges and "neck"tarines!

Why did the vampire
bite Indiana Jones?

He had a taste for
adventure.

I got stung by
a bee yesterday . . .

. . . It charged me ten
quid for a pot of
honey.

Why is Dracula a
hopeless goalkeeper?

He hates the
crosses.

How do I stop people being rude to me?
Who cares, you stupid idiot?

● ● ● ● ● ● ● ● ● ●

What game do mice like the best?
Hide and squeak!

How do you stop a mole digging up the garden?

Hide the spade!

● ● ● ● ● ● ● ● ●

What's worse than being a fool?

Fooling with a bee!

● ● ● ● ● ● ● ● ●

How far can Egyptian fish swim?

A NILE and a half!

# BEANObooks Competition

## Roger is a Dodger, Minnie is a Minx, but Dennis is a ...................................!

Complete the sentence and put your answer in the box below and you could win a great BEANObooks prize in the monthly **BEANObooks prize draw!** A winning name will be drawn from the postbag and published in The Beano comic in the first issue of every month.

A BEANObooks prize will also be awarded to the best joke sent in every month. A prizewinning joke will be picked from the postbag every month and printed in The Beano comic.

Send your entry to:
BEANObooks Competition, P.O. Box 305, London, NW1 1TX.

### BEANObooks Competition

First Name..............................    Answer......................................

Surname..................................    My Favourite Joke...................

Address...................................    ............................................

............................................    ............................................

............................................    ............................................

Postcode................................    ............................................

Contents may change

## AND LOOK WHAT YOU GET!
- BEANO PLAYING CARDS • COOL T-SHIRT
- GIANT POSTER • 64 PAGE MAGAZINE • TOTE BAG • NOVELTY PRACTICAL JOKE

# THE BEANO CLUB MEMBERSHIP REQUEST
Call FREEPHONE 0800 413 877 or visit The Beano website at www.beanotown.com

**PLEASE PRINT CLEARLY IN INK**

First Name ............................................. Surname ...............................................

Address ..................................................................................................................

Postcode ...............................................................................................................

Phone No. ........................................... Date of Birth ............./............./............

                                                           Day      Month    Year

☐ Boy   ☐ Girl

**T-shirt size**

| Junior | | To fit height | Senior | | Chest size |
|---|---|---|---|---|---|
| a.) ☐ small | | 122-128cm | a.) ☐ medium | | 100cm |
| b.) ☐ medium | | 134-140cm | b.) ☐ large | | 110cm |
| c.) ☐ large | | 148-152cm | c.) ☐ extra large | | 120cm |

Remittance (Sterling only. Do not send cash).Cheques and Postal Orders made payable to D. C. Thomson & Co., Ltd. I wish to pay by Visa/Mastercard/Switch; please charge to my account. My card number is

| | | | | | | | | | | | | | | | | | | |
|---|---|---|---|---|---|---|---|---|---|---|---|---|---|---|---|---|---|---|

Valid from   [  /  ]     Expiry date   [  /  ]     Switch Card Issue No. if applicable ☐ ☐

Card holder's signature .............................................................................

Parent/Guardian's signature (if under 15) .............................................

Tick box if you do not wish to receive special offers or promotional material from selected companies ☐